MACDONALD STARTERS

Spiders

Macdonald Educational

About Macdonald Starters

Macdonald Starters are vocabulary controlled information books for young children. More than ninety per cent of the words in the text will be in the reading vocabulary of the vast majority of young readers. Word and sentence length have also been carefully controlled.

Key new words associated with the topic of each book are repeated with picture explanations in the Starters dictionary at the end. The dictionary can also be used as an index for teaching children to look things up.

Teachers and experts have been consulted on the content and accuracy of the books.

Illustrated by: Richard Orr

Editors: Peter Usborne, Su Swallow, Jennifer Vaughan

Reading consultant: Donald Moyle, author of *The Teaching of Reading* and senior lecturer in education at Edge Hill College of Education

Chairman, teacher advisory panel: F. F. Blackwell, general inspector for schools, London Borough of Croydon, with responsibility for primary education

Teacher panel: Elizabeth Wray, Loveday Harmer, Lynda Snowdon, Joy West

© Macdonald and Company (Publishers) 1971
Third Impression 1974
Made and printed in Great Britain by Purnell & Sons Limited
Paulton, Somerset

ISBN 0 356 03846 7
First published 1971 by
Macdonald Educational
St Giles House
49–50 Poland Street
London W1

I have found a big spider.
It is in the bath.

1

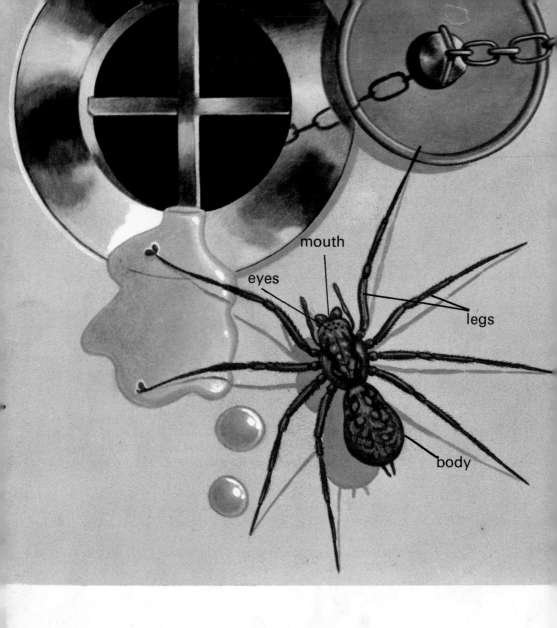

mouth

eyes

legs

body

The spider has eight legs.
It has lots of eyes too.
2

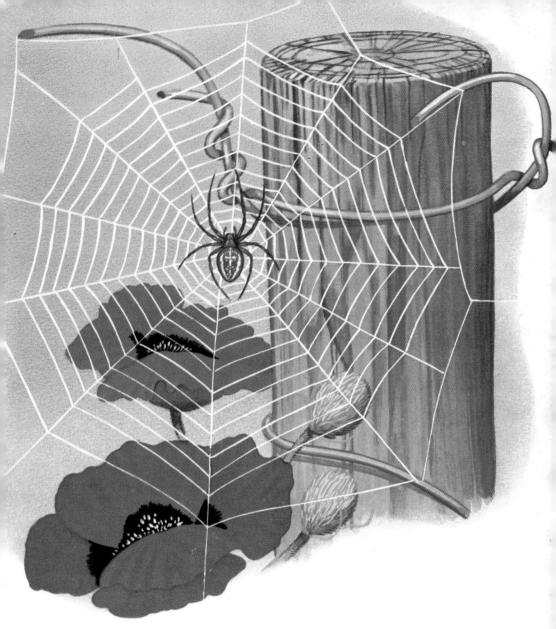

This spider has made a big web.
It waits on the web.

A fly has bumped into the web.
The web is sticky.
The fly cannot get away.

4

Now the spider can eat the fly.
Sometimes spiders wrap flies in web.
The spider can eat the fly later.

A wasp flies into the web.
Wasps often eat spiders.

6

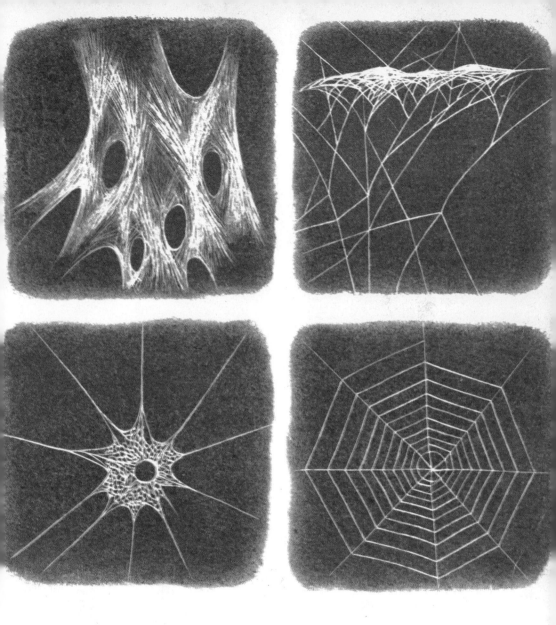

There are lots of different
kinds of webs.

Spiders lay eggs.
Sometimes spiders make round beds
for their eggs.
They are called cocoons.

8

Cocoons are made out of web.
Some spiders carry their cocoons about.

Baby spiders hatch out of the eggs.
Each baby spins a thread.
The baby spiders hang on to the threads.
10

The wind blows the baby spiders.
They hang on to their threads.
They fly like balloons.

11

This spider's leg has broken off.
Now it has only seven legs.
Soon a new leg will grow.

12

Something has frightened the spider.
It is pretending to be dead.

13

This spider jumps.
It does not make a web.
The spider jumps on flies
and other insects.

Another spider digs a hole.
It makes a door with earth and web.
The spider opens the door
and waits for insects.

15

Some spiders hide.
Crab spiders sit in flowers.
They choose flowers
the same colour as their bodies.
16

Another spider lives with ants.
It walks on six legs.
It pretends to be an ant.

This is a very big spider.
It can eat small birds.
18

This spider is called a Black Widow.
It is very dangerous.
It lives in America.

Some spiders live under water.
They make tents.
They take air to the tent.
20

A few spiders walk on water.
They hunt for insects and tadpoles.

shrew

hedgehog

toad

bird

Some animals eat spiders.
All these animals eat spiders.

22

Starter's **Spiders** words

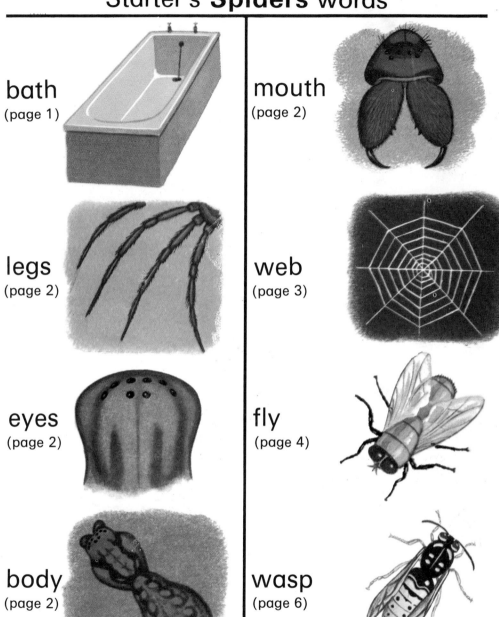

bath
(page 1)

mouth
(page 2)

legs
(page 2)

web
(page 3)

eyes
(page 2)

fly
(page 4)

body
(page 2)

wasp
(page 6)

eggs
(page 8)

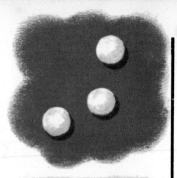

thread
(page 10)

nest
(page 8)

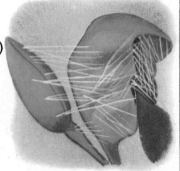

fly
(page 11)

carry
(page 9)

hole
(page 15)

spin
(page 10)

door
(page 15)

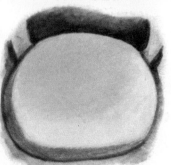

24

flower
(page 16)

bird
(page 18)

crab
spider
(page 16)

Black
Widow
spider
(page 19)

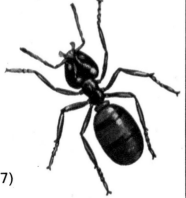

ant
(page 17)

tent
(page 20)